Scariest Places on Earth

THE BIGFOOT TRAIL

By Therese Shea

 Gareth Stevens
PUBLISHING

Please visit our website, www.garethstevens.com. For a free color catalog of all our high-quality books, call toll free 1-800-542-2595 or fax 1-877-542-2596.

Library of Congress Cataloging-in-Publication Data

Shea, Therese.
The Bigfoot Trail / by Therese Shea.
 p. cm. — (The scariest places on Earth)
Includes index.
ISBN 978-1-4824-0928-4 (pbk.)
ISBN 978-1-4824-1142-3 (6-pack)
ISBN 978-1-4824-1141-6 (library binding)
1. Sasquatch — Juvenile literature. I. Shea, Therese. II. Title.
QL89.2.S2 S54 2014
001.944—d23

First Edition

Published in 2015 by
Gareth Stevens Publishing
111 East 14th Street, Suite 349
New York, NY 10003

Designer: Katelyn E. Reynolds
Editor: Therese Shea

Photo credits: Cover, p. 1 RubberBall Productions/Vetta/Getty Images; cover, pp. 1–24 (background texture) Eky Studio/Shutterstock.com; cover, pp. 1–24 (creepy design elements) Dmitry Natashin/Shutterstock.com; p. 5 David Muir/Photographer's Choice/Getty Images; p. 7 (bigfoot trail map) Mkauffmann/Wikipedia.com; p. 7 (USA map) Uwe Dedering/Wikipedia.com; p. 9 Anna Fiorella/USDA Forest Service; p. 11 Jeff Banke/Shutterstock.com; p. 13 (inset) Justin Kral/iStock/Thinkstock.com; p. 13 (main) USDA Forest Service; p. 15 (inset) Eduard Kyslynskyy/iStock/Thinkstock.com; p. 15 (main) spirit of america/Shutterstock.com; p. 16 Audrey Snider-Bell/Shutterstock.com; p. 17 J. Malone/Wikipedia.com; p. 19 (inset) Jupiterimages/liquidlibrary/Thinkstock.com; p. 19 (main) Feargus Cooney/Lonely Planet Images/Getty Images; p. 21 Jordan Siemens/Digital Vision/Getty Images.

Printed in the United States of America

CPSIA compliance information: Batch #CS15GS: For further information contact Gareth Stevens, New York, New York at 1-800-542-2595.

CONTENTS

Words in the glossary appear in **bold** type the first time they are used in the text.

A CLOSE ENCOUNTER?

You're walking through a forest in California. You hear something moving nearby. Crunch . . . crunch . . . Suddenly, you remember you're hiking the Bigfoot Trail. Could it be a *real* Bigfoot?

Bigfoot, also known as Sasquatch, is the name for any large, hairy, humanlike creature that walks on two legs. Some people believe in them, while others don't. Bigfoots are thought to live in the forests of North America. California's Bigfoot Trail may be a perfect home for these creatures!

FRIGHTENING OR FUN?

A Bigfoot is said to be taller than any person and have a rotten smell. In most reports, Bigfoots leave people alone, but other reports say they have thrown rocks at people!

SASQUATCH CROSSING

You might see a sign like this on the Bigfoot Trail of California. Keep your eyes open for these hairy creatures!

A LONG, LONG TRAIL

The Bigfoot Trail takes hikers about 400 miles (644 km) through northwestern California. This distance is so long that it covers six **wilderness** areas and one national park. The trail begins in the south at the Yolla Bolly–Middle Eel Wilderness and ends at the Redwood National Park to the north.

Much of this **route** is so wild that no one tried to complete the whole hike for many years. Instead, they hiked certain sections. At least one hiker, Michael E. Kauffmann, completed the trail in 2009.

The Bigfoot Trail has steep mountains, rushing rivers, and overgrown paths. Michael Kauffman had to cut his way through parts of the Bigfoot Trail. This is called bushwhacking.

Bigfoot Trail

Oregon

Red Buttes Wilderness

Smith River

Klamath River

Siskiyou Wilderness

Happy Camp

Seiad Valley

Yreka

Crescent City

Klamath River

Marble Mountain Wilderness

Scott River

Russian Wilderness

Redwood Creek

Salmon River

Redwood National Park

Willow Creek

Trinity Alps Wilderness

Eureka

Trinity River

Redding

Sacramento River

Eel River

Mad River

Hayfork

Yolla Bolly-Middle Eel Wilderness

Wilderness
National Park
- - - Bigfoot Trail

YOLLA BOLLY—MIDDLE EEL WILDERNESS

The Bigfoot Trail begins in the Yolla Bolly–Middle Eel Wilderness. In the Wintun Indian language, *yo-la* means "snow covered," and *bo-li* means "high **peak**." "Middle Eel" is taken from Eel River, which is found there. The river doesn't contain eels, but does have lamprey—fish that suck other fish's blood!

Most of this wilderness is located in the Mendocino National Forest. The highest point is Mount Linn, which rises 8,092 feet (2,466 m). This mountain is home to the rare foxtail pine tree.

The Yolla Bolly–Middle Eel Wilderness became part of the National Wilderness **Preservation** System in 1964.

FRIGHTENING OR FUN?

Foxtail pines grow above 7,000 feet (2,134 m) on the south side of a mountain! They would die out without places to grow like Mount Linn.

TRINITY ALPS WILDERNESS

The Trinity Alps Wilderness is a long hike north from Yolla Bolly–Middle Eel Wilderness. This area is home to high mountains, deep **canyons**, beautiful meadows, and the Salmon and the Trinity Rivers.

This may sound peaceful, but hikers have to be careful not to **attract** black bears. They put their food in containers so the bears can't smell it. Hikers shouldn't run from bears. These animals can run faster than 30 miles (48 km) per hour! Instead, hikers should back away slowly and wave their arms.

FRIGHTENING OR FUN?

Hikers have to visit Trinity Alps Wilderness during a warm time of year. Some trails get up to 12 feet (3.7 m) of snow in winter. It may not melt until June!

The Trinity Alps Wilderness is so big that it contains over 500 miles (805 km) of trails.

11

MARBLE MOUNTAIN WILDERNESS

The Marble Mountain Wilderness Area is named for Marble Mountain, which contains white **limestone**. The region is one of the oldest protected wilderness areas in California. Besides the mountains there, hikers can enjoy fishing in 89 lakes.

Even if you don't see Bigfoot on this part of the trail, you might see an angry wolverine! Wolverines are the largest members of the weasel family of animals. They have powerful jaws, sharp claws, and the ability to kill animals much larger than they are.

The "Marbles" are part of the larger Klamath Mountains. Today, only people on horseback or on foot can take on the trails of the Marbles mountain **range**. No cars or trucks are allowed.

angry wolverine

13

RED BUTTES WILDERNESS

As hikers keep moving north up Bigfoot Trail, they reach Red Buttes (BYOOTS) Wilderness. A butte is a type of hill with a flat top and steep sides. This wilderness is home to two tall buttes that have a reddish-orange glow because of the metals iron and magnesium in the rock.

Most of Red Buttes Wilderness lies within the Rogue River–Siskiyou National Forest. In this region, too, people claim to have seen Bigfoot. One man saw a Bigfoot swinging from branch to branch. Another said he saw a baby Bigfoot!

FRIGHTENING OR FUN?

Among the scary animals found in the Red Buttes are bats that live under rocky overhangs!

Red Buttes Wilderness crosses into Oregon but is mostly located in California. Rogue River is shown here.

SISKIYOU WILDERNESS

The Bigfoot Trail heads southwest from the Red Buttes Wilderness to the Siskiyou Wilderness. This area is marked by forested hilltops, rocky peaks, and mountainsides covered with brush. The Siskiyou Wilderness has about 20 kinds of conifers. These are trees that have needles and produce cones.

The Siskiyou Mountains cross the wilderness, making it tough for people to fully explore the area. What a great hiding place for Bigfoot! It's definitely home to rattlesnakes, so watch out for those **fangs**!

This is the rare Brewer's spruce, a conifer found in the Siskiyou Wilderness. It's also called the weeping spruce because of the way its branches hang.

FRIGHTENING OR FUN?

Rattlesnakes are **venomous**. Some rattlesnakes in the wilderness have lost their noisy tail, so you may not hear their warning rattle!

REDWOOD NATIONAL PARK

The end of the Bigfoot Trail takes hikers through the Redwood National Park. Redwoods are very tall trees with reddish bark. The tallest redwood on Earth towers 379.1 feet (115.6 m). Redwoods take a long time to grow. Some are thought to be more than 2,000 years old.

The last stop for hikers is Crescent City, California, on the Pacific Ocean. Hikers aren't likely to see Bigfoot here. However, it's a great place to get supplies in case you want to turn around and do the trail again!

FRIGHTENING OR FUN?

In recent years, mountain lions have been seen in Redwood National Park. It's important to never hike alone as these killer cats are more likely to attack a single hiker.

Many of the redwood trees of California have been destroyed by people. Places like the Redwood National Park help keep the remaining trees safe.

TAKE A HIKE!

When Michael Kauffmann hiked the whole Bigfoot Trail, he had to swim across rivers, climb over mountains, and cut down plants in his way. It's definitely not a trail for beginners. Hurt or lost hikers can find themselves miles from help.

Kauffmann hopes that more parts of the trail will be **maintained** by forest services. Maybe someday, the Bigfoot Trail will be as well traveled as other famous trails. If it is, we might find out if Bigfoot is really out there!

Bigfoot Trail might sound scary, but it's an exciting route through a beautiful part of the United States. There are dangerous animals out there, so never hike alone or without an adult!

GLOSSARY

attract: to draw nearer

canyon: a deep valley with steep sides

fang: a long, pointed tooth

limestone: rock formed from skeletons and shells of sea creatures

maintain: to care for something by making repairs and changes when needed

peak: the pointed top of a mountain

preservation: the action of keeping a place safe for animals and plants

range: a line or row of mountains

route: a way, path, or road for traveling from one place to another

venomous: able to produce a liquid called venom that is harmful to other animals

wilderness: a piece of uninhabited land left to grow wild

FOR MORE INFORMATION

Books

Champion, Neil. *Wild Trail: Hiking and Camping*. Mankato, MN: Smart Apple Media, 2013.

Krensky, Stephen. *Bigfoot*. Minneapolis, MN: Lerner Publications, 2007.

Websites

Bigfoot Trail
conifercountry.com/Bigfoot_Trail/
Take an online walk along the Bigfoot Trail using the photos on this site.

How Bigfoot Works
science.howstuffworks.com/science-vs-myth/strange-creatures/bigfoot.htm
Check out this site before you decide if you believe in Bigfoot.

Locations for Plant Explorations in Conifer Country
www.conifercountry.com/nwCalifornia/blog-map.html
Learn more about the plants of the wilderness areas in this book.

INDEX